Contents

Introduction

Planning a wedding can feel pretty overwhelming at times (trust me, I do it for a living). While couples often hire a professional to help manage their wedding plans, there are plenty of reasons why they might also opt to take on the majority of the responsibilities on their own, too. Maybe you're working with a tight wedding planning budget or maybe you simply love all of the DIY possibilities in any case, it's a lot of extra details, but it is possible to plan the wedding of your dreams on your own.

Organization is key to keeping everything on track when you're faced with decisions, lists, deadlines, and everyday life to deal with. The first step is making sure to give yourselves plenty of time for wedding planning. A longer timeline is your friend here aim for around a year, if possible. And don't forget to involve your significant other in this step, as well. Your wedding should represent both of you, together as a couple. So, where to begin? We've got you covered. Just remember to keep one very important thing in mind: Try to have some fun! This is your wedding after all. Don't get too hung up on the tiny details and focus on what's truly important: celebrating the love the two of you share and getting married, all while surrounded by your friends and family.

Your wedding will likely be the biggest party you'll ever throw and figuring out how to plan a wedding can feel pretty daunting at first. But whether you want a small, simple wedding or a big, lavish affair, the steps remain the same: Set a budget (a critical first step!), find inspiration, start your guest list... well, we break it all down one step at a time below. We recommend focusing on one task at a time so you don't get overwhelmed by the wedding planning process. And if you're in a time crunch, go ahead and delegate some of these responsibilities to family members and friends, they'll likely be glad to help you as you navigate this process.

Honestly, there's no hard and fast rule, as you can really mold the steps below to your own timeline slowing down or speeding up (we've even got a three-month wedding checklist) where it works. How much time you need all depends on two important factors: 1) the general timeframe, think year and season, that you want to be married, and 2) how long you want to be engaged. The average engagement length is 13 months, which is totally enough time to tackle the below. If you're someone who finds a wedding checklist a bit overwhelming, here's a list of the basic steps you'll need to complete to ensure your big day is a success. Of course, there are more tasks you may want to tackle, but we're just talking the must-dos here. Ready to go into planning mode? Here's how to plan a wedding step by step.

Wedding planning

Things You Should Know Before You Plan Your Wedding

You're tackling your wedding-planning checklist, diving headfirst in to budgets and guest lists, and making your way through all the other initial steps that are essential in making your wedding the most amazing day ever. Whether you're doing it solo with just the help from your soon-to-be spouse, you have an entire fleet of bridesmaids and in-laws on your side, or have tapped a professional wedding planner, tried and true advice from the people that know best is always welcome, particularly when it makes organizing the many details a little bit easier.

We've asked some top wedding planners, photographers, and florists to share pointers that they wish all couples knew before they started planning. Consider this an insider's guide to planning a wedding with ease. The tips that follow will make the months leading up to your big day easier for everyone across the board, including your vendors.

Remember, it's important to keep the big picture in mind as you contemplate the little details. These expert-approved suggestions will help you make every necessary wedding-planning decision. And since this guide covers everything from when's the right time to book your venue and how to be the very best clients to helpful pointers that will ensure you keep everything perspective, you'll be well on your way to planning the ultimate celebration once you're finishing reading.

Without further ado, click through here for the planning tips experts agree you need to know. You'll want to read and heed the recommendations before you get knee deep into seating charts, napkin colors, and first dance songs.

Don't book your venue before you hire a planner.
Venue selection is the starting point, but if you are able to work with a planner, involving them first can be a lifesaver. "Overall, an experienced planner can assess the venue for logistical and design needs that a couple may not know to look for," says Beth Helmstetter of Beth Helmstetter Events. "This can help not only set realistic expectations upfront, but also to avoid surprises later." Some surprises a seasoned pro can help you navigate through: timing, power, and costs. Most venues won't discuss power with a couple unless the questions are asked, but a planner can help you consider related costs up front so you can avoid financial surprises (and power outages) later on.

Trust your vendors.

The more you trust your vendors and the creatives that you bring on board, the more you will enjoy your wedding. Hire people you like and let them do what they do best. Choosing professionals that can think on their feet and roll with the punches is key.

Patience is a virtue.

Things take time and, believe it or not, you're probably not the only bride your vendor is working with. Bids take time to generate, planners are often waiting on the schedule of other vendors to get you information. And sometimes, other clients are in front of you on our to-do lists. Treat everyone with kindness and respect their business hours and personal boundaries. Aside from being a wedding vendor, everyone is a human being with personal lives.

It's better if you're not aware of everything.

There's a lot that goes on behind the scenes that brides and grooms don't know about and it's better that way. Herculean efforts go into creating a seamless affair. This is not child's play, nor for the meek, nor a vanity project but rather a military op wrapped in a gorgeous box with a bow on top. On any given wedding day, there are (literal) disasters that we deftly maneuver around and quietly dismantle, which is a testament to hard-won experience; we are an insurance policy every bride deserves.

The day is about both of you.
You're getting married, not having a birthday party. Remember: Your wedding is about two people coming together and the celebration should reflect that. Stop comparing your wedding to what your friends have done in the past, what you see on Pinterest, and what your friends and family are telling you need to do. It has to be what feels true to you as a couple. If it means having 1,000 red balloons because it reminds you of your first date, by all means, have the balloons and don't let anybody tell you it's stupid. Don't worry what people think or say about your wedding.

Fighting during planning doesn't mean you're bound for divorce.
It's not weird to fight with your fiancé while working through your wedding planning list of to do's. You're

stressed out after all. Women and men problem solve very differently, so it takes a bit of getting used to. For most couples, this is the first time you will have all of your friends and family in the same place. It's a lot of pressure.

Let it go.

Don't sweat the small stuff. As soon as the wedding day is in progress, brides and grooms have this 'ah-ha' moment where in retrospect they see which decisions were a big deal and which were nothing to worry about this whole time. Listen to your wedding planner who already has the hindsight to know what to prioritize and emphasize versus what not to fret about.

Skip it, who cares

Traditions exist for a reason, but who ever said they were mandatory? If the thought of a first dance with all eyes on you makes you uncomfortable, then don't have one, or start your own tradition. Or perhaps you've never been a cake person but are a longtime fan of glazed donuts. Stack the holey sweets on a pedestal, and bite into one together instead of cutting into a multi-tiered fondant-covered confection.

Unplug. Everyone, unplug.
Who would you need to call if everyone you love is in one place? Put your phone away, and encourage your guests to do the same during the ceremony. Insisting on a cell-phone free ceremony allows your guests to be fully present, instead of being more concerned with snapping mediocre pics during your vows, or getting in your photographer's way to snap a pic of the bride and groom walking down the aisle.

Get in motion.
If you can swing hiring a videographer, do it. In the moment, it seems like a great place to save money if you are trying to figure out how to plan a wedding on a budget, but in the end, all of my clients who passed on videography regret it after the fact.

Not everything costs money.
The same goes at a wedding. Where often, the most crowd-pleasing aspects of a wedding can be free. A

beaming couple, rehearsed first dance, or hand-written vows have an endearing effect guests won't forget.

The Stages of Planning a Wedding
You have finally found the person you want to commit to spending the rest of your life with. It has been something you've always wanted. Now the day has come that you need to start planning a wedding. And unfortunately, unless you're a professional events planner, this can be overwhelming and, at some points, extremely stressful.

Planning for a Wedding
Just the thought of starting a to-do-list can be a lot to take. Let's face it, there are a million things to do, and there's no way of knowing where or how to even start. And don't worry, every soon-to-be bride and groom feels this way. It's a common problem to experience, and it shouldn't ever be something to feel discouraged about. This is a complete guide on how to start planning a wedding, in an organized, calm, and relaxed way.

Stage 1 of Planning a Wedding

Before even starting to plan anything, you need to confirm a few details to help guide you towards making sensible decisions for your future event. These are factors that you first need to confirm before you can start planning a wedding.

Confirm your budget

Before anything else, you need to know what amount of money you'll be working with. It'll be very difficult to plan anything without first confirming the budget you will have for your wedding. It's important to work with an amount that you are 100% sure of.

It is even better to use an amount that you currently have, rather than one that you're expecting to earn later on. This is to guarantee that there are no financial factors that will hinder or change your plans once you start planning a wedding.

Confirm your desired wedding dates or season

The next step is confirming the dates you desire to work around for your wedding. This can be specific, or it can be a certain season. You should consider what type of theme you're looking to have if you're planning on the dates. For example, if you want a tropical beach theme, then you need to plan a wedding during the summer season.

Factors to consider when choosing a wedding date:

1. Give yourself the time to plan: Unless you are looking to have a really simple wedding, you'd want to give yourself at least 6 months to plan. The ideal time to plan would be around 6 months to a year. The more time you have planning a wedding, the easier and relaxed the process will be. It'll also give your guests the time to take time off of work or obligations, and commit to your date.

2. Choose a date when everyone's available: As much as possible, it is best to have your wedding date land on a weekend or a time when you know people will have time off of work. It'll be easier for everyone if you do this. You can also get the input of your close family and friends, to get a good idea of what dates are best to choose from.

3. Avoid national holidays: As tempting as it is to plan on a national holiday (assuming everyone will be available), this can be a risk. Vendors and venues may be closed for the holidays. Your guests may have prior commitments. It's just not a good idea.

Identify a theme and do a little research
After knowing what dates you're planning to have your wedding on, and having a good idea of the budget you're willing to dish out for your wedding, it's time to do a little research and brainstorming. You'd want to get a good idea of what theme you're aiming to have at your wedding. This can be a rustic, tropical, vintage, and even a simple garden theme.

Once you have a good idea of the type of theme you want, you can then start looking into research. This includes venues, catering, flowers, music, cake, and pretty much everything you'll need on the day. This doesn't have to be detailed and extensive research. It's just a way to get an idea of what you can and can't have at your wedding. Keep your budget and dates in mind when you do your research.

Don't forget to include the opinion and wants of your partner too. This may be obvious, but not everyone does this. This will guarantee that both of your preferences will be represented at your wedding.

Stage 2 of Planning a Wedding
This is the stage when the real planning for a wedding begins. It's when you start to pull all of the foundations of your event, from the planner, to the guest list, to the venue, together. This all needs to be done before you can move on to even start considering the food and everything else.

Hire a planner
Hiring a planner is completely optional, but it is also strongly advised. The problem with weddings that do not have planners, is that both the bride and groom and their entire entourage end up experiencing the bulk of the stress and exhaustion that comes along with planning a wedding. This results in the entire wedding party feeling significantly tired on the actual wedding day.

You need to hire a planner that you know will be able to accommodate your needs and will prioritize what you want, over what they have experience with.

Factors to consider when hiring a wedding planner:

1. Experience: A lot can go wrong at a wedding, and only an experienced wedding planner will have the knowledge to anticipate and resolve a problem. Make it a point to check that they have had a lot of experience planning for a wedding. It'll also be a big advantage if they have experience planning a wedding that's similar to the one you want to have.

2. Accommodating to your preferences: Once you start talking about what you and your partner want on your special day, it's important to take note if your wedding planner helps give you tips to achieve your preferences, or if they are discouraging of your ideas, and are insisting on their own. You need a planner who will be there to take care of your needs, but also, who will also respect what you want on your wedding day.

3. A personality you can work with: No matter how good your wedding planner is, their personality can make the biggest difference in the outcome of your wedding. You want to be able to plan your wedding with someone that you enjoy working with. It may not seem like a big deal at first, but it will be a significant factor when you experience the stress of planning a wedding with this person.

4. Must be local to your area: It'll be easier working with a wedding planner who is local to your location. They will have a good idea of what it's like where you live. They'll know all of the local vendors and venues. And they will be able to anticipate the weather and any other possible hindrances that may affect your wedding day.

Start the guest list
The next step is starting your guest list. Don't get this wrong. This isn't the final guest list for your wedding. It is more of an estimate of how many people you're aiming to accommodate at the event. You need this to move on to the next steps of planning a wedding.

Look for a venue

With the number of guests in hand and an idea of the date, it's time to consider what venue will work around this and your budget. If you have a venue in mind, this is the time to arrange a viewing. Know the capacity of guests at the venue. Check the available dates. It's important to have your wedding planner with you so that they can confirm if your desired venue will be able to accommodate the production of a wedding. This includes parking, lighting, tables and chairs, a stage, and a sound system. Your planner will be able to help you out with this process, but it'll also be good for you to be present to see the venue for yourself.

Reserve the venue

As soon as you are happy with the venue, and your wedding planner has confirmed that it can work for your wedding, then it's important to reserve this as soon as possible. Venues can often be booked out up to a year or two ahead of time. It's important to put a deposit down to reserve your date as soon as you possibly can, to guarantee that you have reserved the dates you want.

Once you have, you can move on to the next stage of planning a wedding.

Reserving a venue also includes reserving the church or venue for your actual marriage ceremony. Again, take into consideration the number of people, and the accessibility of this place (this includes parking).

Stage 3 of Planning a Wedding
This is the stage of planning a wedding when you can start building the structure for your actual wedding day. This includes your decorations, the food, the cake, your dress, and all the small details that will fill the venue and your wedding day's festivities.

Plan for the catering
If your lucky enough to have a venue that provides catering, you need to confirm what food is available for your wedding. You also need to plan a taste test. If you want a private catering company to handle your reception, you'll need to explain what type of food you would want on your wedding day. Planning for a wedding means trying everything for yourself before

letting your guests experience the food. What you need to discuss with the caterers:

1. The number of guests: Let the caterers know the estimated number of guests that you need to cater for. This is to guarantee that your catering will be able to accommodate your entire guest list.

2. The meal options: Not everyone will like the dish you choose for yourself. It's safe to have an option of meat, fish, and a vegetarian dish, for your guests to choose from. You'd want to be able to provide for everyone's preferences.

3. Plan a taste test date: Choose the dishes that you'd be happy to have at your wedding, and arrange for a taste test. It's a good idea to have 2 choices of meat, 2 choices of fish, and 2 choices of vegetarian food. This will allow you to choose what dish tastes better. You should also taste the desserts and/or drinks they are planning to serve.

4. Confirm if they cater for alcohol too: You'd want to be able to provide wine, champagne, and other liquor at your wedding. Confirm if your venue or

catering service provides this, or if you will have to hire a separate vendor for the booze at your wedding.

Find a cake maker
Your caterers may be able to recommend a good cake maker for your big day. But it's always best to find the cake maker that suits you and your preferences. Remember, when you're planning for a wedding, it's less about what everyone else wants, but rather, what you and your partner want. And choosing the right cake maker is an important part of planning a wedding.

If you're not particularly fussy about your wedding cake, then you can choose an affordable bakery to make you a multi-tier cake for your reception. If you are particular about your desserts, then you can request for a taste test to get a good idea of the flavors you can choose from.

Plan for the decorations
You'd want to have great decorations for your wedding day. Once you're done planning for the catering, you can have a good idea of how to plan for your decorations. This includes everything from flowers, lights, table

settings, food displays, and everything else that'll add to the visual aesthetic of the venue. The decorations are another big part of planning a wedding.

This is a crucial part of planning for a wedding as you will not be able to do this for yourself. Instead, you will be relying entirely on the collaboration of your wedding planner's team and your catering team. You need to set your instructions and make them clear.

Find the right dress or dressmaker
It's now time for one of the best moments for every bride to be. Finding yourself the perfect dress or meeting the right dressmaker. You may already have a good idea of what you want for your wedding dress. If you don't, it's okay too. This is the time to go out and explore what options you have locally. If you're looking for a dress:

1. Go to a dress boutique: It's better to be able to fit a dress, to see if it looks good on you. And going to a boutique will give you the chance to try different types of dress styles, colors, lengths, and fabrics.

2. Avoid buying a dress on the Internet: Buying a dress online won't allow you to fit it on yourself. And not everything that's posted online, reflects the real quality of a product. It's not a good idea to buy your wedding dress on the Internet.

3. Set a budget for your dress: It's easy to get carried away with the amount of money you plan to spend on your dress. You need to first set a budget for your dress so that you do not commit to spending on a dress that in the end, you can't afford. You may find that you run out of money if you're not planning a wedding with your budget in mind.

If you're looking for a dressmaker:

1. Ask for their price range: Different dress designers will have different prices. It all depends on what market they are catering to. When you meet possible designers, immediately disclose the amount of money you have for a dress. This will help you avoid wasting each other's time.

2. Research your choice of designers: You want to go for a designer that has experience working with your body type, who has good feedback from previous brides, and who has a good experience.

3. Try to work with a local designer: To get the absolute perfect fit, the altercations and changes to the dress can happen just days before your actual wedding day. Your body will go through changes, and you will need to have a designer who will be close to you/your venue. This will make it easier for you to see them whenever you want to get re-measured.

Find the right Suit or Suitmaker

Take your partner to get his suit made, or to fit suits, the same way you are planning to have your dress done. It's also important that the suit fits him well. That he is comfortable in it as he will spend almost an entire day wearing this. Finding a suit will not be as time-consuming as the dress, but it is still a good idea to give him enough time to choose the suit that he is happy with.

Plan your entourage's attire

As you have confirmed you and your partner's outfits, it's time to talk about your entourage's clothes. You need to plan this alongside your entourage. You have to know what they are comfortable wearing. Or if you have outfits in mind, you need to let them be aware of it. If you're looking for a dress:

1. Go to a dress boutique: It's better to be able to fit a dress, to see if it looks good on you. And going to a boutique will give you the chance to try different types of dress styles, colors, lengths, and fabrics.

2. Avoid buying a dress on the Internet: Buying a dress online won't allow you to fit it on yourself. And not everything that's posted online, reflects the real quality of a product. It's not a good idea to buy your wedding dress on the Internet.

3. Set a budget for your dress: It's easy to get carried away with the amount of money you plan to spend on your dress. You need to first set a budget for your dress so that you do not commit

to spending on a dress that in the end, you can't afford. You may find that you run out of money if you're not planning a wedding with your budget in mind.

If you're looking for a dressmaker:

1. Ask for their price range: Different dress designers will have different prices. It all depends on what market they are catering to. When you meet possible designers, immediately disclose the amount of money you have for a dress. This will help you avoid wasting each other's time.

2. Research your choice of designers: You want to go for a designer that has experience working with your body type, who has good feedback from previous brides, and who has a good experience.

3. Try to work with a local designer: To get the absolute perfect fit, the altercations and changes to the dress can happen just days before your actual wedding day. Your body will go through changes, and you will need to have a designer

who will be close to you/your venue. This will make it easier for you to see them whenever you want to get re-measured.

Find the right Suit or Suitmaker
Take your partner to get his suit made, or to fit suits, the same way you are planning to have your dress done. It's also important that the suit fits him well. That he is comfortable in it as he will spend almost an entire day wearing this. Finding a suit will not be as time-consuming as the dress, but it is still a good idea to give him enough time to choose the suit that he is happy with.

Plan your entourage's attire
As you have confirmed you and your partner's outfits, it's time to talk about your entourage's clothes. You need to plan this alongside your entourage. You have to know what they are comfortable wearing. Or if you have outfits in mind, you need to let them be aware of it.It can be expensive to have your whole entourage's clothes custom made, so it's usually a common practice for brides and grooms to either ask their entourage to buy their clothes with a request of a color theme. Or there's

also the choice of buying ready-made dresses and suits, and just have them altered to fit each person perfectly.

Plan the attires for:

- Maid of Honor
- Best Man
- Bridesmaids
- Groomsmen
- Flower girls
- Ring bearer
- Bible bearer
- Coin bearer
- Parents
- Primary and Secondary Sponsors

It doesn't matter what approach you take, but it is a good idea to plan for these outfits all ahead of time.

Create your invitations
With the venue, the menu, the date, and the event coming together, you can now officially create your invitations. This is the time that you confirm all of the guests you plan to have, give them the options for your meals on the

day, and share all of the exciting details of your wedding day.

You can build invitations with your wedding planner to guarantee that all of the necessary details are present in your invites.

Hire a photographer and videographer
A common aspect that people tend to leave at the last minute of planning a wedding, is hiring a photographer and videographer. It is really important to have a professional team handling the documentation of your special day.

You don't have to hire an expensive photography and videography team if you don't want to dedicate too much of your budget to this aspect of your wedding. You can hire a local photographer, maybe even support someone who is just starting in the industry. What's important is to have someone who can take the photos and videos you'd want of your wedding day.

Give your photographer and videographer a brief idea of everything you're planning for your wedding, to give them a good idea of what they should prepare to cover. This includes your venue, the color theme, the season, and the number of guests you are expecting.

Hire a host for your wedding reception
Having a host for a wedding may not be something you're considering to have. But it is really important. You need someone who can organize your wedding and all of the activities of the reception and to overall control your guests, the timing of the event, and everything that's happening. It's a good idea to have a host who knows you well.

Hire a DJ or a band for music
Having the right type of music at your wedding will set the ambiance you want. You need to consider what type of songs you'd like to have at your wedding. It'll be great if these are songs that both you and your partner enjoy.

This is around the time that you should be hiring a DJ or a band. When planning for a wedding, you wouldn't want to leave this too late as entertainers are booked ahead of time. And you wouldn't want to find yourself without the band or DJ that you want, hosting the music for your special day.

Plan for your transportation
You need to book for a wedding car as soon as possible. This is the car that will take you to the church, to the reception, and then back home after the wedding. You need to hire a driver and a car as you may not have the time to get anyone to drive you to the church. You also wouldn't want to drive yourself there with such a wedding dress. If possible, you should also try your best to arrange the transportation of your entourage so that you can guarantee that they are all on time before you walk down the aisle. It'll also be nice to have them by your side throughout the event.

Book hotel rooms (if necessary) for you and your entourage
If you're not using your own home, you should also be booking a hotel room or accommodation for you, your groom, and your entourage, for the wedding day. You will all be working with the same designers and makeup and hair artists, and it's always a good idea to have everyone under one roof.

Stage 4 of Planning a Wedding

You are just a few weeks away from your wedding, and these are the final details that you need to confirm and arrange for before the big day.

Register for gifts

If you haven't already, it's time to register for gifts, so that your guests have the time to choose what gifts they can give you on your big day. When you register for gifts, you can make it easier on everyone and do this through an online store. Lucky for you, many of the big department stores offer their wedding gift registration services online.

Create a Timeline for the Wedding Day

With everything booked and in place, you must not forget this important factor when planning for a wedding. You and your wedding planner need to confirm the timeline of the entire event. You need to do this to be able to give this information to everyone involved. The catering, the production team, the church, the venue, the host, the entertainers, the decorators, they all need to know the gist of the timing of everything at your wedding. This will help keep things organized and stress-free.

Plan for your rehearsal dinner
Your rehearsal dinner is really important as you need to give your entourage the chance to understand what will happen during the event. With a lot of people involved, organization and synchronization are important.They need to know what they should be doing at that time. Your wedding planner will not have the time to guide and direct people's directions. And a rehearsal dinner will be what everyone needs to get all the timing and obligations correct.

Finalize seating plan
You need to finalize seating plans to give to the wedding planner who will organize all of this on the wedding day. Of course, this is optional. But it will be a lot more organized if people have seats allotted to them.

Confirm all of your bookings
This is more of a job for your wedding planner. You need to confirm everything at least 3 days before your actual wedding day. Make sure every vendor and service

are reminded of your day and their obligations. Once you have confirmed all of this, you will be happy to move on to preparing yourself for the big day.

Top tips for how to plan your wedding

Set Your Wedding Budget—and Stick to It

Your wedding budget will be the driving factor for many of your wedding-related decisions, so this should be one of the first things you tackle. If any family members will be contributing, chat with them about what they're comfortable spending. If you're footing the bill yourself, it's time to take a hard look at your finances. Be prepared for a reality check when it comes to actually budgeting for your wedding day as many couples don't realize the full scope of costs involved. Once you've got that magic number, stick to it!

Construct a List of Wedding Day Priorities

Sit down with your partner and determine what the three most important aspects of your wedding will be. Is it the venue or specific wedding date? Locking in a certain wedding photographer or live band? Prioritize those details and be willing to compromise on the rest. This will help you stay within your budget and help you focus your efforts on what really counts.

Determine Your Bridal Style
Find a few resources of bridal inspiration you like best, Pinterest, Instagram, magazines, trusty bridal sites (including Brides, of course!) and start researching. Having a good sense of the type of wedding style you want helps immensely once you start meeting with potential vendors. Don't overwhelm yourself with all the wedding inspiration that's out there. Creating one or more Pinterest boards or even a visual collage on a cork or poster board will help you to figure out what sort of look and feel you really want and keep you aligned with your larger vision.

Get Organized
You can use checklists, spreadsheets, Word, Excel, Google Docs anything, really as long as you can gather all your thoughts, budgets, numbers, etc., in one place. There are also some great online tools and apps out there

that can keep you organized. We love WeddingHappy for staying on track with tasks and AllSeated for visualizing seating charts and venue layouts.

Involve Your Significant Other
Don't feel like you're in this wedding planning process alone. Consult with your partner along the way; their opinion is bound to be invaluable and even if they're only involved in some aspects, it makes wedding planning that much more fun when you can make decisions together. Working towards a common goal not only further bonds you and your partner but also helps you grow as a couple with every issue you tackle as a team.

Buy a Wedding Planning Book
For couples who opt to take on the wedding planning process sans a professional planner or coordinator, a traditional etiquette and guidebook (such as The Wedding Book) is a wealth of information and expert advice, including tips and tricks and even examples of timelines and checklists.

Create a Master Checklist

Check out our master wedding-planning checklist and timeline to keep yourself on track and tackling tasks like a pro. (Feel free to adapt it to suit your own needs, as necessary). This will help you visualize and prioritize goals without being overwhelmed with everything all at once.

Bouquet toss

Your wedding should be all about the two of you as a couple. If certain traditional aspects make you uncomfortable, feel outdated, or simply aren't your style, then just don't include them on your wedding day. Traditions are lovely, but only when they're meaningful to you. taking videos during the ceremony, have the officiant make a quick announcement before proceedings begin.

Make It Legal

In the midst of all the crazy planning and endless small details, don't forget to actually plan time to get your marriage license. Start researching and gathering the necessary documents early on, but keep in mind that marriage licenses are typically only valid for a couple of months and destination weddings often have their own stipulations, so plan accordingly.

Postpone Honeymoon Planning

Simultaneously planning a wedding and a dream honeymoon is not only expensive but also very time consuming. Especially if the two of you are doing everything yourselves. It may be a good idea to postpone honeymoon planning just a bit. Many couples recommend spacing out the wedding and honeymoon to really appreciate everything, rather than being too drained from the wedding planning to fully enjoy the post-nuptial getaway.

Allocate Toasts and Readings

Wedding toasts are typically reserved for select VIPs and are traditionally distributed between the rehearsal dinner and reception, though some couples choose to have everything take place at one event. You are responsible for notifying toast-makers of their responsibilities, accepting requests to speak, and organizing the speaking order. Including readings in the ceremony, whether traditional, cultural, or literary, is a great way to honor important people in your lives that aren't part of the wedding party. As with toasts, you assume responsibility for choosing the speakers and defining the speaking order.

Finalize Setup Details

As your wedding date approaches, check in with your venue to find out when your vendors can arrive for setup. The earlier the better, but in some cases, venues may have other events going on the same day. Be sure to pass along the information to your vendors so everyone is on the same page.

Build a Playlist

Regardless of if you are having a live band, DJ, or manning the turntables yourself, you will need to outline all of the key songs that absolutely must be played during the nuptial festivities. Just as important: Don't forget to also create a list of the songs you definitely don't want to hear.

Write Vows

Take off your wedding planner hat for just a moment and don your to-be-wed headdress. Indulge yourself in a few moments of solitude to gather your thoughts and put pen to paper as you conceive the declarations of love and nuptial pledges you will make to your spouse-to-be as you are married. Make sure to include some actual promises in your notes rather than just creating a love letter to your beloved. They are called vows for a reason, after all.

Produce a Schedule of Events

Creating a comprehensive wedding day schedule ensures everyone is on the same page about timing and location(s) and helps to make sure the day's events run smoothly. Include things like hair and makeup appointments, when vendors will arrive, timing for transportation to/arrival at the ceremony location, timing for the couple's arrival to the reception, speeches and the first dance, when the cake will be cut, etc. Print out (or email) copies to your MC, photographer, maid of honor, key family members, all vendors, and anyone else that should be in the know.

Say Thanks

Gratitude goes a long way. Be sure to arrange for small gifts for your wedding party and anyone else who played a big role in your wedding planning journey including friends who pitched in to help with all of your wedding DIY projects and, of course, parents or other family members who have been there for you and supported you along the way. Don't hesitate to give them a special little shoutout during the wedding toast, too.

Most Common Wedding-Planning Mistakes Couples Make

Top event designers (with a combined 121 years working in weddings) reveal the blunders, pitfalls, and missteps many couples make during the planning process. Read about them now accompanied by photos of real weddings that got it right so you can avoid them later!

Making Plans Before Setting a Budget

Picking a dress or wedding venue prior to establishing financial parameters is a lot like shopping without glancing at price tags and then strolling up to check out with your fingers crossed. You risk falling for a gown or location that breaks your heart when you realize that to afford it, you'd have to cut your guest list in half or cancel the honeymoon. "The three initial hurdles are budget, guest list, and venue, and they should be tackled in that order," says planner Lynn Easton of Easton Events in South Carolina and Virginia. "Your budget defines your options and drives your decisions." While drawing one up, "include charges for overtime, gratuities, and car services from the start," advises New York City planner Marcy Blum. "By doing so, you avoid throwing money at things you weren't prepared for."

Not Having a Rain Plan
If yours is an outdoor event, rain on your wedding day isn't just ironic, it's a game-changer. Too many people are tempted to just hope it won't happen, which is the planning equivalent of sticking your fingers in your ears and yelling, "I can't hear you, Rain! People don't want to put the deposits down for tents, umbrellas, and golf carts they might not need, you pay 50 percent and lose it if you don't use them. But if you don't book them early on

and are marrying during peak wedding season, tents might not be available when the weather starts to look iffy. Meet with the tent company six to nine months ahead and think of the deposits as an investment in your peace of mind. We believe that if you have a good Plan B, it won't rain, but if you haven't considered 'what if,' it will undoubtedly pour.

Underestimating the Cost of Outdoor Affairs
Just because the setting may be breezy doesn't mean the planning is going to be easy. With alfresco affairs, people think we're just putting a tent in a field, and it's going to be beautiful. They don't realize all the logistics necessary for a tented event to go off without a hitch." Bear in mind you'll need to rent bathrooms, kitchen facilities, lighting, fans or heaters, and generators.

Planning a Too-Long Party
It's the event of your lifetime, but it shouldn't feel like it lasted a lifetime. It's tempting to get so excited that you map out a marathon celebration, with pre-vow drinks, a lengthy ceremony, another cocktail hour, a multi-course dinner, three hours of dancing, an after-party, and more.

But industry insiders agree that a five-hour reception is the tip-top of what people can enjoy and still exit laughing. The evening should have a natural end. It should also have a comfortable beginning: Be sure to supply chairs so attendees can sit for the vows (a five-minute ceremony becomes a painful 20-minute wait if you run late).

Packing Them In
You want your wedding to feel chic and elegant, not "crowded elevator." Being cramped makes meal service and dancing difficult, and it really inhibits the guest experience. Ask your venue how many attendees can comfortably fit, then reduce that by 10 percent. You don't want to get to the max of what your site can accommodate."

Mistiming Vows
Schedule your ceremony to get the best photos. Figure out when the sun goes down, then chat with your photographer about the ideal start time. There is a 'golden hour' just before the sun sets that photographers

love to take advantage of. Think of it as nature's airbrushing; you just have to make an appointment for it.

Not Supplying Enough Information
No one likes feeling confused, and your guests won't know the wedding locale the way you do. Offer suggestions of things to do and information on getting around, and if you're having a destination event or weekend-long celebration, hand out itineraries telling everyone where they need to be and when. That way, the buses won't be late to the vows because no one knew when or where they needed to be picked up. Speaking of buses, give the drivers their fair share of need-to-know info too. I can't tell you how many times I've told a transportation company what the address is, and they still get lost. Now we print out directions describing exactly the way we want them to go so we can estimate how long it will take to move guests from place to place.

Micromanaging
Drawing a map for the bus drivers is a great idea. Plotting out bathroom breaks and a second-by-second schedule for your coordinator, waitstaff, and DJ? Not so

much. Folks forget they're dealing with seasoned professionals who can forecast down to the nano-second how the party should go. Be clear about what you want, but know that offering trust and creative license to your team produces a better end result for all involved.

Skipping Video
Yes, the movie version of your big day will go months or even years between viewings, and videography is a tempting place to cut costs. However, Nothing compares to being able to relive your wedding in real time; it goes by in a flash. Our clients always call us to gush over the details the next day, and it's hard to hear when their only regret is not having hired a videographer.

Sweating the Small Stuff
Your brother may forget to bring the programs you spent last weekend hand-stamping, your mom may insist on leading a conga line at the reception, and your father-in-law may call your boss "honey" when they're introduced. But who cares? You're marrying the love of your life! Too often we see couples get so wrapped up in the details that the focus shifts from the celebration of a

marriage to a fixation on the 'stuff' of a wedding. It's hard to have fun and be present in this once-in-a-lifetime moment if you're worried the peonies in the centerpieces are one Pantone shade off.

Rushing to Register
Already picturing yourself scanning everything in sight at your favorite store? There's plenty of time for you to go scanner crazy later, but think it through first. You'll save yourself the disappointment of wanting a registry do-over. So many couples describe their registry experience as stressful and uninspiring. Your registry should be the foundation of the home you'll build together. Register somewhere that offers real design assistance, ideally with someone that shares your sensibility. With the help of a pro you'll be able to set your couple style and pick pieces you'll keep forever.

Signing a Catering Contract That Lacks Detail
Catering is likely the largest financial contract you'll sign and the most crucial when it comes to creating your wedding experience. The person who promised you something might be long gone by the time your wedding

comes around. Get everything in writing. Always check for (or add) these things to your contract: staffing for waiters, bartenders, and support staff; alcohol varieties and brands; what food/courses are included and what counts as an upgrade (and how much it costs); and access for setup/breakdown and any additional charges.

Making it an Open-Mic Night
Heartfelt toasts can be the highlight of a reception, but too many can quickly lead to wide-spread boredom. Oftentimes, speakers intend to speak only for a few moments, but once onstage their speeches can last quite a while. We're looking at you, fathers of the bride. Keep control of your event by limiting toasts to the host, maid of honor, and best man, staggering toasts throughout dinner, and having a quick chat with your DJ or band leader to avoid any surprises.

Underestimating the Importance of Stationery
Your save-the-dates and invitations shouldn't be an afterthought when it comes to your wedding style. They may seem less important because there are a few months between the save-the-dates and invitations and the big

day, but it's these two items that gives guests the first impression of what to expect. Setting the right tone from the beginning helps create a more cohesive event. Working with a professional stationer or a calligrapher to get the look you're going for.

Trying to Please Everyone
Of course you want your family and friends to have fun, but ultimately it's your wedding. Worrying too much about what other think of your decisions will take the joy out of the wedding-planning process and the focus away from what everyone is really celebrating,. As long as there's enough food, proper temperature control, and plenty of seats, you know your guests are well taken care of. Anything beyond that colors, dresses, décor, venue is all about you!

Thinking That at Least 10 Percent of Guests will RSVP "No"
It's a commonly shared stat that you can expect at least 10 percent of your guest list to RSVP "no." While that may be the rule-of-thumb, it's not an exact science. And this can mean big problems for your budget or space if

you've booked a venue that holds 200 but invited 240 with the expectation that 40 people will skip the festivities. No one can guarantee how many guests will RSVP and how many won't until invites go out. The only way to truly keep your guest count and budget manageable is to limit your number of invitees.

Being Blinded by Tradition
It's great to stick to some wedding traditions if you like them, but don't feel obligated. If you just follow along and do what you think you're supposed to do, you'll end up with a wedding that says nothing about who you are. What makes each wedding special is the bride and the groom that are being celebrated. If tradition is important to you, infuse it with your personal style and attitude." With this simple tip in mind you'll create a wedding that shows off your family traditions while also reflecting your personality.

Conclusions

However much you don't want to think it, something could go wrong on the day. This could be anything from a problem with the catering to rain (despite the forecast promising a dry day). Plan alternatives for each scenario and account for anything that might not go to plan so you're not left stressed out and panicking on the big day. Additionally, you should invest in wedding insurance, and check what circumstances are covered under your policy.

Everyone wants to look fab in their wedding photos, so if you'd like a confidence boost, now's the time to adopt a healthy eating plan and practise a few simple exercises to tone your body. On the other hand, going on an extreme diet is definitely not a good idea. Just remember that your groom wants to marry you exactly the way you are!

This should be everything you need to do when it comes to planning for your wedding. You do not necessarily have to follow this guide word-by-word. But it's a good reference to have when you ever feel overwhelmed or if you think you might just be missing something. Keeping your plans organized will give you the chance to truly enjoy every second of your wedding day, without ever having to worry about a thing.